USDA

United States
Department of
Agriculture

Forest Service

Pacific Southwest
Research Station

General Technical Report
PSW-GTR-223
August 2009

Residents' Responses to Wildland Fire Programs: A Review of Cognitive and Behavioral Studies

James D. Absher, Jerry J. Vaske, and Lori B. Shelby

Authors

James D. Absher is a research social scientist, U.S. Department of Agriculture, Forest Service, Pacific Southwest Research Station, 4955 Canyon Crest Drive, Riverside, CA 92507. **Jerry J. Vaske** is a professor, Colorado State University, Human Dimensions of Natural Resources, Fort Collins, CO 80523. **Lori B. Shelby** is an assistant professor, George Mason University, School of Recreation, Health, and Tourism, Manassas, VA 20110.

This report is a collaborative effort among the U.S. Department of Agriculture, Forest Service, Pacific Southwest Research Station; Colorado State University, Human Dimensions of Natural Resources Department; and George Mason University, School of Recreation, Health, and Tourism.

Abstract

Absher, James D.; Vaske, Jerry J.; Shelby, Lori B. 2009. Residents' responses to wildland fire programs: a review of cognitive and behavioral studies. Gen. Tech. Rep. PSW-GTR-223. Albany, CA: U.S. Department of Agriculture, Forest Service, Pacific Southwest Research Station. 31 p.

A compilation and summary of four research studies is presented. They were aimed at developing a theoretical and practical understanding of homeowners' attitudes and behaviors in the wildland-urban interface (WUI) in relation to the threat from wildland fires. Individual studies focused on models and methods that measured (1) value orientations (patterns of basic beliefs) toward natural processes, (2) attitudes toward wildland fire policies, and (3) behavioral intentions to adopt defensible space activities or support agency policies/actions. This report presents some of the key findings from these studies, highlights the practical consequences of adopting a theory-based approach to understanding wildland fire management in urbanized areas, and suggests strategies for successful wildfire-prevention education programs.

Keywords: Wildland fire, behavioral intentions, fire beliefs and attitudes, firewise actions.

Introduction

Recent wildfires in the Western United States highlight the need for understanding the human dimensions of forest and wildfire management. The U.S. Department of Agriculture Forest Service (U.S. Forest Service) Pacific Southwest Research Station in collaboration with Colorado State University's Human Dimensions of Natural Resources Department, the Colorado State Forest Service, and the Larimer County, Colorado, government, has been an active participant in contributing to the growing body of knowledge related to the human dimensions of wildfire management.

This report (1) reviews some of the key findings from four research studies (see app. 1 for methodological details on each study), (2) highlights the practical consequences of adopting a theory-based approach to understanding wildland fire management in urbanized areas, and (3) presents strategies for successful firewise[1] programs.

Conceptual Foundation

Popular media commonly assert that values influence environmental attitudes and behaviors, but empirical evidence showing direct predictive validity is sparse (Stern 2000). Social-psychological theories offer explanations for these disparities, suggesting that attitudes and beliefs mediate the relationships between values and behavior (Whittaker et al. 2006). These theories distinguish stable but abstract values (Homer and Kahle 1988, Rokeach 1973) from more specific cognitions (e.g., attitudes) that evaluate objects or situations encountered in daily life (Eagly and Chaiken 1993). These cognitions are best understood as part of a "hierarchy" from general to specific. Specific belief or attitudinal variables are more likely to predict behaviors than more general measures like values or value orientations (fig. 1). Our research has applied this "cognitive hierarchy" to predict public acceptance of support for wildfire management policies (Absher and Vaske 2007a, 2007b) and homeowners' willingness to adopt defensible space activities (Absher and Vaske 2006).

---

[1] Throughout this paper we refer to firewise in its generic sense, and do not intend to refer to the national FireWise program explicitly.

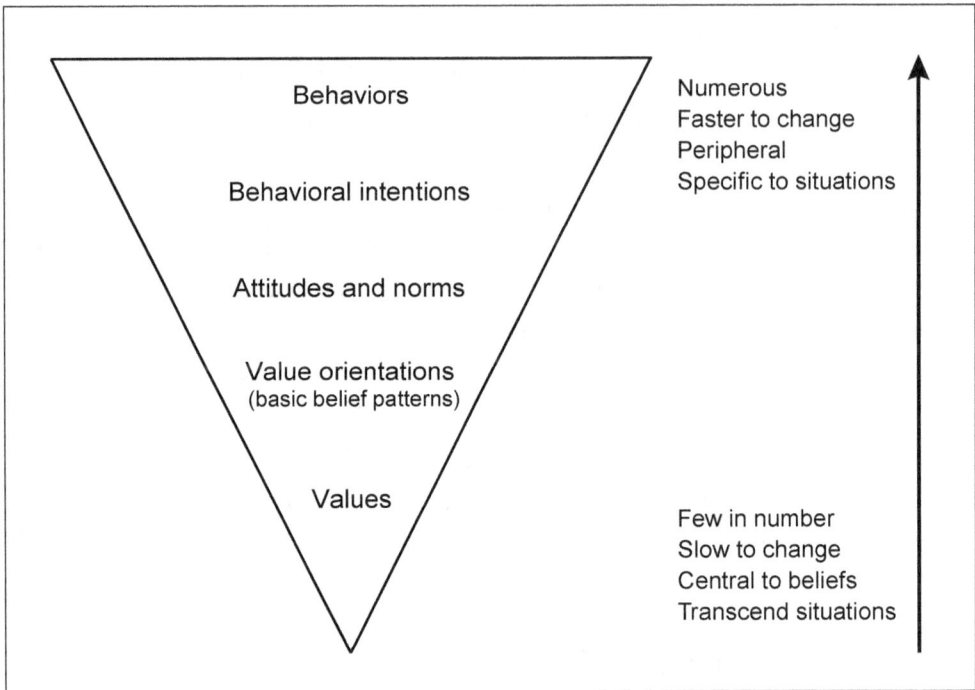

Figure 1—The cognitive hierarchy (Source: Vaske and Donnelly 1999).

Concepts Measured

Beliefs and Value Orientations

The studies reviewed in this report developed and tested various measures important to understanding homeowners' actions in the face of risk from wildland fire. In particular, these studies focused on (1) value orientations (patterns of basic beliefs) toward natural processes, (2) attitudes toward wildland fire agencies and their policies, and (3) behavioral intentions to adopt defensible space activities or support agency policies/actions.

Basic beliefs emerge from and give meaning to fundamental values. Our research (Absher et al. 2008; Bright et al. 2003, 2005) has identified five basic belief dimensions related to perceptions of wildfire management. Table 1 illustrates the reliability of these dimensions across visitors to three national forests (Arapaho-Roosevelt in Colorado; Mount Baker-Snoqualmie in Washington; and San Bernardino in California). Although not exhaustive, these basic beliefs represent key value-based dimensions that underlie public perceptions of wildfire management issues. Cronbach's alpha was used to gauge the internal consistency of survey responses associated with each concept. This coefficient ranges from 0 to 1 with alpha levels greater than 0.70 typically considered to be a reliable reflection of the concept.

Basic beliefs represent key dimensions underlying wildfire management.

2

Table 1—Reliability coefficients for basic beliefs across studies

Study	Basic beliefs[a]				
	Biocentric	Anthropocentric	Responsibility	Freedom	Trust
Arapaho-Roosevelt NF[b]	0.86	0.77	0.73	0.78	0.83
Mount Baker-Snoqualmie NF[b]	.87	.77	.72	.73	.77
San Bernardino NF[b]	.85	.77	.57	.74	.78

[a] Cell entries are reliability coefficients (Cronbach's alpha).
[b] Bright et al. 2003, 2005; Absher et al. 2008.

The first two dimensions replicate biocentric and anthropocentric basic belief dimensions identified in the literature (Vaske and Donnelly 1999). A **biocentric** dimension reflects the extent to which the health and welfare of ecosystems and their components (e.g., habitat and wildlife) are of primary concern in natural resource and environmental management. An **anthropocentric** basic belief reflects the extent to which humans are of primary concern regarding natural resource management. The alpha coefficients for the biocentric scale ranged from 0.85 to 0.87 for the three study areas. The coefficients for the anthropocentric scale revealed a similar pattern of findings. The consistency of these findings for both scales provides an initial validation of the scales.

The next three dimensions trace directly to the work of Rokeach (1973). As applied to wildfire management issues, the **responsibility** basic belief focuses on who is responsible for protecting homes built in or near the WUI and who is responsible for managing the risk of wildfire (e.g., private landowners, public agencies, both). The **freedom** basic belief dimension refers to the extent that private landowners should be free to or constrained from building private residences in or near the WUI where wildfire may occur. Finally, the **trust** basic belief dimension reflects the extent to which the public "trusts" the ability of public agencies to effectively manage wildfire. Across the different study areas, reliability coefficients for these dimensions were consistent and substantial ($\alpha = 0.72$ to 0.83); the only exception was the alpha ($\alpha = 0.57$) for responsibility reported by San Bernardino respondents.

Table 2 contains the specific items associated with each dimension and introduces another basic belief from the risk literature, **salient value similarity** (SVS). It comprises both a sense of what is important (salient) in a particular setting and the extent to which relevant actors (e.g., agencies, neighbors) share those values in meaningful ways, especially with respect to the establishment of trust (Cvetkovich and Winter 2003).

Table 2—Reliability analysis of basic belief dimensions for combined studies

Belief dimension/item[a]	Mean	Standard deviation	Cronbach alpha
Biocentric:			0.86
Nature has as much right to exist as people.	2.19	1.44	
Forests have as much right to exist as people.	2.12	1.46	
Forests have value whether people are present or not.	2.70	0.81	
Wildlife, plants, and people have equal rights.	1.69	1.77	
Anthropocentric:			.77
The value of forests exists only in the human mind.	-2.31	1.44	
Nature's primary value is to provide products useful to people.	-1.64	1.69	
The primary value of forests today is to provide places to play and recreate.	-1.37	1.67	
The primary value of forests is to provide timber, grazing land, and minerals for people.	-1.41	1.69	
Forests are valuable only if they produce jobs and income for people.	-2.45	1.03	
Responsibility:			.70
Homeowners are responsible for protecting their homes, near a forest, from wildfire.	-0.86	1.84	
Community fire department is responsible for protecting homes built near a forest from fire.	-0.10	1.70	
The government agency that manages the forest is the most responsible for protecting homes built near a forest from wildfire.	-0.27	1.73	
When people build homes near forests, it is their own fault if their home is damaged by wildfire.	-0.31	1.79	
When people build homes near forests, they have the right to expect their home will be protected from wildfire by the government agency managing the forest.	-0.55	1.76	
If a wildfire breaks out in a forest, the first priority of the agency managing that forest is to make sure private property is not destroyed.	-0.39	1.86	
Freedom:			.80
People should be allowed to build homes where they want, even if it is in a high-risk wildfire area.	0.23	2.25	
People should not be allowed to build near forests where their homes could be destroyed by fire.	-0.99	1.82	
Laws should prohibit building homes where they can be burned by wildfires.	-0.84	1.86	
Trust:			.79
Prescribed burning is an appropriate management tool.	-1.47	1.39	
Prescribed fire is too uncontrollable to be a forest management tool.	-0.87	1.47	
Forest managers should not use artificial methods (prescribed fire) to manage forest fires.	-1.03	1.54	
Salient value similarity:			.95
With respect to forest fire management, I feel that the U.S. Forest Service:			
Shares similar values as me.	0.86	1.56	
Shares similar opinions as me.	0.63	1.57	
Thinks in a similar way as me.	0.49	1.59	
Takes similar actions as I would.	0.46	1.65	
Shares similar goals as me.	0.69	1.59	

[a] All items coded on a 7-point scale: (-3) strongly disagree to (+3) strongly agree.

The results indicated that, in general, people had a moderately strong agreement with a **biocentric** view (means of 1.69 to 2.70) and a weak or negative stand toward **anthropocentric** positions (means of -2.45 to -1.37). **Responsibility, freedom and SVS** averaged near the middle of the scale suggesting that people were split across the spectrum of opinions (means of -0.99 to 0.86). The generalized **trust** items showed a moderately low average level of agreement (means of -1.47 to -0.87).

In addition to the general trust questions (table 2), we also measured trust relative to (1) trust in the U.S. Forest Service management and (2) trust in U.S. Forest Service information (table 3). Questions associated with both concepts showed moderately strong levels of agreement across all items (means of 0.82 to 1.76) and strong Cronbach's alphas ($\alpha = 0.76$ and 0.93, respectively) when combined into indices.

Table 3—Reliability analysis of wildfire related trust dimensions and attitudes

Belief dimension/item[a]	Mean	Standard deviation	Cronbach alpha
Trust management:[a]			0.76
I trust that the U.S. Forest Service knows how to:			
Effectively plan prescribed burns	0.82	1.71	
Use mechanical thinning effectively	1.17	1.60	
Respond to forest fires	1.68	1.37	
Trust information:[a]			.93
With respect to forest fire management, I trust the U.S. Forest Service to provide:			
The best available information on forest fire issues	1.58	1.42	
Me with enough information to decide what actions I should take	1.68	1.35	
Truthful information about safety issues related to a forest fire	1.76	1.33	
Timely information regarding forest fire issues	1.51	1.52	
Attitude toward wildfires:			.91
Wildfires are bad (-3) — good (+3)	0.17	1.75	
Wildfires are harmful (-3) — beneficial (+3)	0.50	1.81	
Wildfires are negative (-3) — positive (+3)	0.26	1.64	
Attitude toward prescribed burning:			.82
How effective are prescribed burns in preventing subsequent fires from getting out of control[b]	1.73	1.47	
Do you approve or disapprove of the use of prescribed burns in forests[c]	1.87	1.88	
Do prescribed burns make the forest look better or worse[d]	0.67	2.05	
Attitude toward mechanical thinning:			.81
How effective is mechanical thinning in preventing subsequent fires from getting out of control[b]	1.84	1.58	
Do you approve or disapprove of the use of mechanical thinning in forests[c]	2.04	1.90	
Does mechanical thinning make the forest look better or worse[d]	1.30	1.99	

[a] Responses given on a 7-point scale: (-3) strongly disagree to (+3) strongly agree.
[b] Responses given on 9-point scale: (-4) not at all effective to (+4) extremely effective.
[c] Variable coded on 9-point scale: (-4) strongly disapprove to (+4) strongly approve.
[d] Variable coded on 9-point scale: (-4) extremely worse to (+4) extremely better.

Wildland Fire Attitudes

Our research measured both general and specific attitudes toward wildfire (table 3). The general attitude toward wildfire used a three-item semantic differential scale (i.e., bad–good, harmful–beneficial, negative–positive). The specific attitudes examined attitudes toward prescribed burning and attitudes toward mechanical thinning. These indices included three dimensions (i.e., effectiveness, approval, and visual aesthetics) and used 9-point rating scales with a 0 center point. Results showed slightly positive attitudes toward wildland fire (means of 0.17 to 0.50) and positive attitudes toward prescribed burning (means of 0.67 to 1.87) and mechanical thinning (means of 1.30 to 2.04). When combined into scales, all three attitudes had strong Cronbach's alphas of 0.91, 0.82, and 0.81, respectively.

Linking Cognitive Measures to Behaviors

The cognitive hierarchy provides a theoretical foundation for connecting beliefs to more specific cognitions and behavior. Trust in an agency, for example, has been suggested as a key psychological predictor of public acceptability of management actions. Research suggests that social trust is based on perceived similarity rather than carefully reasoned attributions of trust or direct knowledge of the managing agency (Earle and Cvetkovich 1995, Siegrist et al. 2001, Winter et al. 2004). The adjective "social" emphasizes that the people being trusted are those with formal responsibilities within organizations and may not be personally known to the person making the trust attribution (Siegrist et al. 2000). Social trust affects more specific cognitions such as support for policies or intention to engage in specific personal firewise behaviors. People are predicted to base their trust judgments on whether they share similar goals, thoughts, values, and opinions with the agency (i.e., a basic belief).

The role of social trust in gaining public support is highlighted.

Vaske et al. (2007a, 2007b) predicted that trust mediates the relationship between salient value similarity and attitudes toward prescribed burning and mechanical thinning. A structural equation analysis was used to assess the mediation role of social trust (fig. 2). Results indicated that respondents shared the same values as USDA Forest Service managers (table 2), and trusted the agency to use prescribed burning and mechanical thinning effectively (table 3). As hypothesized, social trust fully mediated the relationship between SVS and attitudes toward prescribed burning and mechanical thinning. As SVS similarity increased, social trust in the agency increased. As social trust increased, approval of prescribed burning and mechanical thinning increased. These findings highlight the role of social trust in gaining public support for wildfire management and are consistent with prior SVS research suggesting that trust mediates the relationship between value similarity and attitudes.

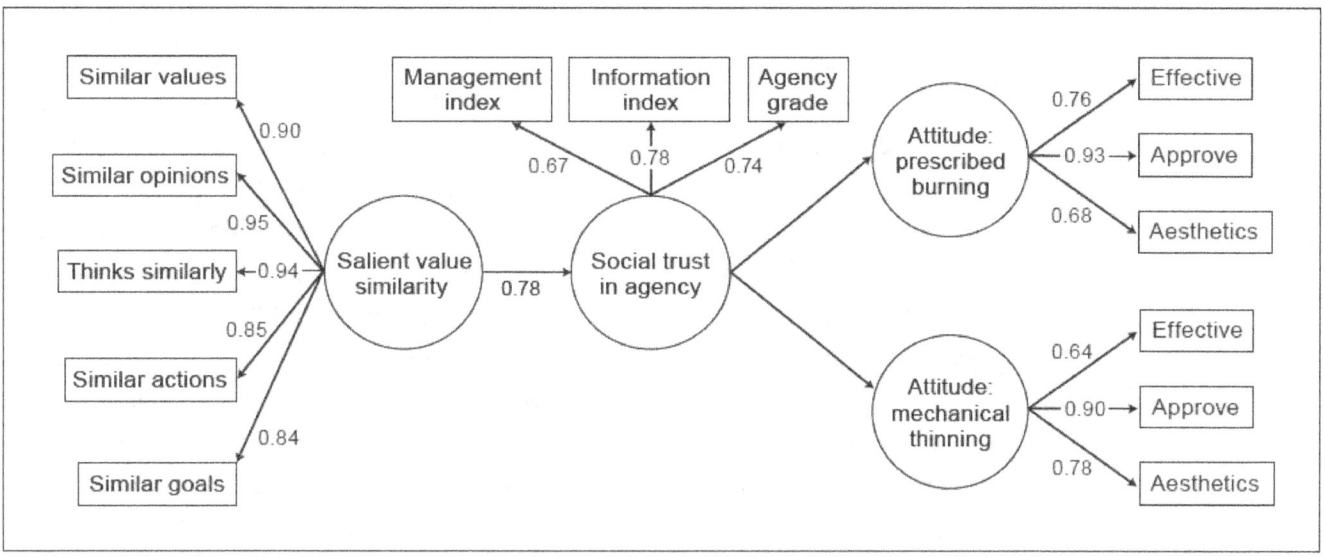

Figure 2—Confirmatory factor analyses and full mediation structural equation model. Note: Path coefficients are standardized regression coefficients. All coefficients are statistically significant ($p < 0.001$).

Predicting Behavior

Past Behaviors and Support for Agency Actions

The effectiveness of an agency's wildfire communication strategies depends on public support (Absher and Bright 2004, Bright et al. 2007, Toman et al. 2008). Combinations of underlying factors influence support for "agency policies" (e.g., prescribed fire, mechanical thinning) and "homeowner behaviors" (e.g., defensible space, firewise construction). Our approach identified three broad categories of predictor variables—sociodemographic, situational, and psychological (table 4).

Sociodemographic variables such as age, sex, education, and income have been shown to be related to residents' perceptions of wildland fires and potential

Table 4—Variance explained by sociodemographic, situational, and psychological predictors across homeowner and agency behaviors

Independent variables	Homeowner behaviors		Agency behaviors	
	Defensible space	Firewise construction	Mechanical thinning	Prescribed burning
Sociodemographic	0.021 (n.s.)	0.017 (n.s.)	0.063 (.042)	0.054 (.004)
Situational	.073 (< 0.001)	.032 (0.021)	.007 (n.s.)	.020 (n.s.)
Psychological	.441 (< 0.001)	.270 (< 0.001)	.390 (< 0.001)	.393 (< 0.001)

Note: Top number in each cell is Nagelkerke R^2 value. Bottom number is significance level (n.s. = not significant).

mitigation strategies. Individuals with more income, for example, have more personal resources to adopt some homeowner wildland fire mitigation strategies (e.g., firewise construction). **Situational variables** define a given context and influence what the public perceives as acceptable or feasible. Large tracts of forested land often surround homes built in the WUI. Proximity of a home to a forest is likely to enhance the homeowners' general awareness of the potential dangers associated with wildland fires and their willingness to accept mitigation efforts. **Psychological variables** include specific beliefs and attitudes regarding wildfires (e.g., perceived familiarity with, or effectiveness and aesthetic impacts of, wildfire or treatments).

These classes of predictors, however, are not likely to contribute equally to homeowner mitigation behaviors or support for agency wildland fire policies. The cognitive hierarchy predicts that **general** sociodemographic variables (e.g., education, income) and **general** situational variables (e.g., location of home) will account for only a fraction of the variability in homeowner wildland fire mitigation strategies and support for agency policies. More **specific** psychological variables (e.g., beliefs about effectiveness, aesthetics of mitigation efforts) are predicted by theory to explain a relatively large amount of the variation.

Table 4 supports these predictions. Sociodemographics had no statistical effect on personal defensible space or firewise construction behaviors and explained less than 6 percent of the variance in support for agency behaviors (mechanical thinning, prescribed burning). Situational variables explained 3 percent to 7 percent of the variability in personal behaviors and had no influence on agency behavior support. Psychological variables (e.g., familiarity, effectiveness, aesthetic impacts), however, consistently predicted both homeowner behavior and support for agency behaviors (R^2 range: 27 percent to 44 percent). Clearly it is very important to understand the role of psychological variables with respect to wildland fire actions.

Predicting Defensible Space Behavioral Intentions

Using a series of hierarchical regression models, we predicted residents' intention to do each of seven firewise actions based on whether they currently do the behavior, their beliefs about the effectiveness of the action, their situational characteristics (property attributes), and sociodemographics (respondent characteristics). Following the logic of the cognitive hierarchy, variables were entered into each model in the following order: (1) currently performs behaviors, (2) perceived effectiveness, (3) property attributes, and (4) respondent characteristics. For each possible firewise action, there were four models. Table 5 shows the change in explanatory power (R^2) and associated statistical probability (F-value, significance) for each model. The pattern of findings was consistent for each of the seven firewise action intentions.

Table 5—Regression models predicting specific defensible space activities[a]

Model	R^2	ΔR^2	ΔF-value	p-value
Clean roof surfaces/gutters surrounding vegetation:[b]				
Model 1: Currently do (X_1)	0.385	0.385	214.62	< 0.001
Model 2: X_1 + Perceived effectiveness (X_2)	.448	.063	38.78	< .001
Model 3: X_1 + X_2 + Property characteristics (X_{3i})[c]	.453	.013	2.78	0.041
Model 4: X_1 + X_2 + X_{3i} + Respondent characteristics (X_{4i})	.454	.008	1.24	0.295
Stack firewood / lumber at least 30 feet from house:[b]				
Model 1: Currently do (X_1)	.576	.576	457.25	< 0.001
Model 2: X_1 + Perceived effectiveness (X_2)	.624	.049	43.61	< 0.001
Model 3: X_1 + X_2 + Property characteristics (X_{3i})	.632	.008	2.31	0.077
Model 4: X_1 + X_2 + X_3 + Respondent characteristics (X_{4i})	.634	.002	.507	0.730
Use nonflammable building material:[b]				
Model 1: Currently do (X_1)	.329	.329	167.85	< 0.001
Model 2: X_1 + Perceived effectiveness (X_2)	.372	.043	23.52	< 0.001
Model 3: X_1 + X_2 + Property characteristics (X_{3i})	.374	.002	.391	0.759
Model 4: X_1 + X_2 + X_3 + Respondent characteristics (X_{4i})	.382	.008	1.15	0.334
Plant fire-resistant plants:[b]				
Model 1: Currently do (X_1)	.332	.332	165.02	< 0.001
Model 2: X_1 + Perceived effectiveness (X_2)	.445	.113	67.60	< 0.001
Model 3: X_1 + X_2 + Property characteristics (X_{3i})	.454	.009	1.72	0.163
Model 4: X_1 + X_2 + X_3 + Respondent characteristics (X_{4i})	.469	.015	2.27	0.062
Plant trees and shrubs at least 15 feet apart:[b]				
Model 1: Currently do (X_1)	.396	.396	217.69	< 0.001
Model 2: X_1 + Perceived effectiveness (X_2)	.468	.072	44.78	< 0.001
Model 3: X_1 + X_2 + Property characteristics (X_{3i})	.476	.008	1.68	0.172
Model 4: X_1 + X_2 + X_3 + Respondent characteristics (X_{4i})	.481	.005	.711	0.585
Prune tree branches within 85 feet of house 10 feet above ground:[b]				
Model 1: Currently do (X_1)	.460	.460	295.54	< 0.001
Model 2: X_1 + Perceived effectiveness (X_2)	.514	.054	38.74	< 0.001
Model 3: X_1 + X_2 + Property characteristics (X_{3i})	.518	.004	.87	0.456
Model 4: X_1 + X_2 + X_3 + Respondent characteristics (X_{4i})	.525	.007	1.20	0.313
Reduce density of trees within 100 feet of house:[b]				
Model 1: Currently do (X_1)	.449	.449	283.73	< 0.001
Model 2: X_1 + Perceived effectiveness (X_2)	.474	.024	16.12	< .001
Model 3: X_1 + X_2 + Property characteristics (X_{3i})	.475	.001	.32	0.811
Model 4: X_1 + X_2 + X_3 + Respondent characteristics (X_{4i})	.482	.007	1.13	0.342

[a] Independent variables:

Currently do = respondent currently does the specific defensible space activity.

Perceived effectiveness = respondent's belief about the specific defensible activity.

Property characteristics = (1) distance from forested area, (2) residence in subdivision (Yes/No), (3) lot size.

Respondent characteristics = (1) sex, (2) age, (3) education, (4) income.

[b] Dependent variable = intention to perform specific defensible space activity in the future.

[c] Lot size was the only statistically significant ($p = 0.020$) property characteristic variable.

Current behavior was always the best predictor of future behavior and explained between 33 percent and 58 percent of the variability. Adding the psychological variable (model 2) to the initial current behavior model consistently increased the amount of explained variance (ΔR^2 range = 2 percent to 11 percent). With the exception of cleaning roof surfaces (ΔR^2 = 1 percent), including the property variables (model 3) did not statistically improve the predictive power of the models. With the other three sets of independent variables in the equations, none of the sociodemographic variables were significant (model 4).

Observations

Variables in each of the three classes of predictors can influence individual homeowner behavior and support for agency policies. Consistent with social psychological theory and the specificity principle, specific wildland fire beliefs and attitudes (i.e., psychological predictors) had more predictive power than either the general sociodemographic or general situational indicators. Engaging residents in doing some type of behavior, no matter how small, provides an important first step to broader adoption of firewise actions. These results point to the utility of knowing the social and psychological precursors of behavior in a community or area of concern. Finally, the relative influence of these predictors differs by specific type of homeowner behavior and agency policy. Sociodemographic variables had more influence in **agencywide** policy models, whereas the situational variables affected only **homeowner** behaviors.

Greater support for agency policies and individual behaviors might be possible if the communication strategy enhances residents' knowledge or understanding of the rationale for them.

Perceived familiarity, effectiveness, and aesthetic impacts (psychological variables) of the agency policies or homeowner behaviors had a strong and consistent influence. This suggests that greater support for agency policies and individual behaviors might be possible if the communication strategy enhances residents' knowledge or understanding of the rationale for them. Thus agencies could enhance compliance with firewise construction and defensible space strategies by paying attention to the psychological drivers and to the situational variables of homeowners such as proximity to the forest. Given the homeowners' costs associated with adopting firewise construction and the potential barriers that these pose to compliance, our results also suggest that residential land developers and the home construction industry could be an important target for communication efforts—especially if they will agree to incorporate firewise principles more often and to market such options to customers more aggressively.

Encouraging Action

Encouraging the public to take action (e.g., creating defensible space) that can reduce the likelihood of wildfire damage in their communities and decrease the likelihood of injury is a common approach to increasing wildfire safety. Communication campaigns have been employed to describe how WUI residents can protect themselves and their homes from wildfire. In northern Colorado, one prominent example of an agency communication effort is Colorado's "Are You Firewise?" program. This information campaign, launched in 1998 by the Colorado State Forest Service in cooperation with Larimer County, Poudre Fire Authority, and Loveland Fire Department includes a package of instructional materials that provide information to residents on how to take steps to be firewise around their home. Included in this information package are a set of flyers that describe seven areas of firewise behavior for WUI residents. Specific topics contained in the flyers include access, water supply, defensible space, trees and shrubs, construction materials and design, interior safety, and what to do when. Table 6 describes the general content of information contained in each topic flyer.

Table 6—Topic descriptions for northern Colorado's "Are You Firewise?" program

Topic	Description
Access	Actions before a fire to enhance the ability of firefighters to locate and get to your home
Water supply	Actions to ensure adequate and accessible sources of emergency water
Defensible space	Actions to modify areas around their residence (clearing or landscaping)
Trees and shrubs	The use and planting of fire-resistive trees and shrubs to create defensible space
Construction	Actions related to use of fire-resistant building materials, design, and locations
Interior safety	Use of sprinklers, smoke detectors, fire extinguishers, and escape plans at home
What to do when	Actions to take when home is threatened by wildfire

Evaluating the effectiveness of agency efforts that focus on persuasive communication is an important aspect of responsible natural resource management (Absher and Bright 2004). Evaluation of current information campaigns is necessary to determine their effectiveness in encouraging behaviors that will ultimately reduce damage caused by wildfire. Understanding how residents of Colorado's WUI react to educational material such as the firewise information flyers can enhance future efforts to communicate important safety information to the public.

One of our studies explored the multiple roles of source credibility in the elaboration and impact of messages about conducting firewise behaviors in the WUI. Our objectives were to examine:

- Whether credibility of the source of information impacts how much WUI residents carefully consider messages about firewise behaviors (especially differences among three agencies: USDA Forest Service, the Colorado State Forest Service, and local fire authorities).
- The extent to which message clarity mediates the credibility-elaboration relationship.
- The moderating effect of message elaboration on the relationship between source credibility and self-reported behavior change.

The conceptual foundation for this study was the **elaboration likelihood model** (ELM; Petty and Cacioppo 1986). The ELM examines the extent to which message-relevant thinking, or elaboration, occurs about the information in a message. Elaboration implies that a person (1) attends to a message; (2) processes the message in light of relevant associations, images, and experiences accessed from memory; and (3) draws inferences and an overall evaluation about the merits of the arguments within a message (Petty and Cacioppo 1986). When an individual elaborates on the content of a message and its arguments, the resulting attitude change occurs through a central route of information processing. When an individual does not elaborate on the information, yet attitude change takes place owing to other factors tangential to the message, the person is using a peripheral route of information processing. Factors that influence a person's motivation and ability to elaborate on information include (1) context factors such as the method with which the information is presented, (2) recipient factors such as working knowledge (Biek et al. 1996), (3) source factors such as credibility (Heesacker et al. 1983), and (4) message factors such as the relevance of the issue described in a message and message clarity (Hafer et al. 1996). For this study, we examined source credibility and message comprehension as they influence elaboration and attitude change.

Source credibility influences the motivation to elaborate on a message. Heesacker et al. (1983), for example, found that message recipients were more motivated to elaborate on information when it was provided by an expert than a nonexpert. Similar findings were found by Manfredo and Bright (1991) in examining the effects of U.S. Forest Service brochures on canoeist behavior in the Boundary Waters Canoe Area Wilderness. Source credibility also serves as a tangential cue to the quality of the message under low elaboration (Petty and Cacioppo 1986). The credibility of message source has been found to be positively correlated to attitude change when factors limit the recipient's ability to elaborate on the message, such as when they are distracted or when issue knowledge is low (Wood and Kallgren 1988).

Message clarity is also positively related to an individual's ability to elaborate on a message. For example, complex messages are often elaborated upon less because it takes more cognitive effort to understand them (Hafer et al. 1996). For a person to consider information, they must understand it.

Firewise Message Effectiveness

For five of the seven firewise information topics (access, construction, water supply, trees and shrubs, and what to do when) examined in this study, there was no significant relationship between source credibility and message elaboration (regression 1) or message clarity (regression 2), and therefore no opportunity for mediation by message clarity to occur (table 7). For the defensible space topic, source credibility was positively related to message elaboration ($\beta = 0.273$, $p = 0.004$) and message clarity ($\beta = 0.174$, $p = 0.048$). For the interior safety topic, source credibility was again positively related to both message elaboration ($\beta = 0.206$, $p = 0.028$) and message clarity ($\beta = 0.189$, $p = 0.050$). A regression was run for these topics to determine if message clarity mediated the significant relationship between source credibility and elaboration. For the defensible space topic, both source credibility ($\beta = 0.229$, $p = 0.014$) and message clarity ($\beta = 0.256$, $p = 0.006$) were significant predictors of message elaboration indicating no mediation occurred. For the interior safety topic, message clarity was a significant predictor of elaboration ($\beta = 0.200$, $p = 0.024$), whereas the relationship between source credibility and elaboration became nonsignificant ($\beta = -0.012$, $p = 0.892$) suggesting that message clarity fully mediated the source credibility/elaboration relationship.

Message elaboration was also regressed on source credibility and message clarity for the other five topics. Message clarity was a significant predictor of message elaboration for access ($\beta = 0.268$, $p = 0.005$), construction ($\beta = 0.309$, $p < 0.001$), trees and shrubs ($\beta = 250$, $p = 0.006$), and what to do when ($\beta = 0.264$, $p = 0.003$). Message clarity did not significantly predict message elaboration for the topic of water supply.

The level of message elaboration moderated the effects of source credibility on behavior change for five of the seven firewise topics. The relationship between source credibility and behavior change was statistically significant for the high-elaboration group yet not significant for the low-elaboration group, suggesting moderation. This occurred for the topics of defensible space ($r = 0.332$, $p = 0.003$ vs. $r = -0.041$, $p = 0.826$), water supply ($r = 0.226$, $p = 0.031$ vs. $r = -0.067$, $p = 0.682$), interior safety ($r = 0.220$, $p = 0.050$ vs. $r = 0.184$, $p = 0.431$), trees and shrubs ($r = 0.338$, $p = 0.003$ vs. $r = 0.180$, $p = 0.235$), and what to do when ($r = 0.360$, $p = 0.002$ vs. $r = 0.127$, $p = 0.594$). There were no significant correlations between source credibility and behavior change by elaboration group for either the access or construction topics.

Table 7—Mediation and moderation analyses for each firewise topic

Firewise topic/ study variables	Objective 1: Mediation of message clarity on the source credibility-elaboration relationship[a]			Objective 2: Moderation of elaboration on the source credibility–behavior change relationship[b]	
	Regression 1 dependent variable: Elaboration	Regression 2 dependent variable: Clarity	Regression 3 dependent variable: Elaboration	Low elaboration group; correlation of source credibility with behavior change	High elaboration group; correlation of source credibility with behavior change
Access:					
Source credibility	0.152	0.157	0.056	-0.081	0.167
Message clarity			.268[c]		
Construction:					
Source credibility	-.032	.140	.013	-.088	.161
Message clarity			.309[c]		
Defensible space:					
Source credibility	.273[c]	.174[c]	.229[c]	-.041	.332[c]
Message clarity			.256[c]		
Water supply:					
Source credibility	.039	.018	.037	-.067	.226[c]
Message clarity			.119		
Interior safety:					
Source credibility	.206[c]	.189[c]	.012	.184	.220[c]
Message clarity			.200[c]		
Trees and shrubs:					
Source credibility	.073	.016	.069	.180	.338[c]
Message clarity			.250[c]		
What to do when:					
Source credibility	.111	.099	.085	.127	.360[c]
Message clarity			.264[c]		

[a] Mediation analyses were conducted following procedures outlined by Vaske (2008).

[b] Moderation analyses were conducted following procedures outlined by Vaske (2008) when both the predictor (source credibility) and moderator (elaboration) are continuous variables.

[c] β (mediation analysis) and r (moderation analysis) are statistically significant at $p < 0.05$.

All agencies were perceived as at least somewhat credible, but the Colorado State Forest Service was perceived as most credible.

Source credibility. One-way analysis of variance was used to determine if the three groups (U.S. Forest Service, Colorado State Forest Service, local fire departments) differed on their perceived credibility for providing information about forest fire and firewise issues. All agencies were perceived as at least somewhat credible in providing information about these topics. The Colorado State Forest Service was perceived as most credible ($M = 6.02$ out of 7.00), statistically higher than the credibility of the U.S. Forest Service ($M = 5.50$) and the organization of local fire departments ($M = 5.68$) ($F = 5.28$, $p = 0.005$).

Compliance with Firewise Recommendations

Respondents were asked to report their compliance with a sample of 26 key recommendations contained in the seven firewise flyers. On average, 53 percent of respondents said that the suggested actions were "already done" on their property. For these questions, respondents were also presented with a "does not apply" option. The proportion choosing this option ranged from 5 percent for "what to do when" actions to 33 percent for water supply actions (16 percent across all topics). These individuals were retained when calculating rates of compliance because some respondents also reported obstacles for some actions, and it is unclear exactly what was meant by "does not apply" in the context of each recommended action. Overall compliance was lowest for "what to do when actions" (34 percent) and highest for access actions (71 percent). Responses to specific actions differed widely from only 2 percent in compliance with the recommendation to have a residential sprinkler system in the home to 92 percent in compliance with the recommendation to have a roof that is constructed of fire-resistant materials (e.g., asphalt shingles, metal). Reported compliance percentages for each topic and action are listed in the topic-specific tables in appendix 2.

Responses to specific actions differed widely from 2 percent to 92 percent compliance.

Prevalence of Obstacles to Implementation of Firewise Recommendations

Respondents reported obstacles across all topics and actions presented in the firewise information flyers. In total, 48 percent of respondents that reviewed firewise information wrote an obstacle statement for at least one of the recommended actions. Content analysis of the open-ended comments revealed 486 total obstacle statements. The most frequently mentioned obstacles to firewise implementation were cost of carrying out actions and disagreement with the utility of actions. These obstacles were reported 125 and 47 times, respectively (table 8). The cost obstacle was also mentioned by the largest percentage of respondents (21 percent).

The most frequently mentioned obstacles to firewise implementation were cost of carrying out actions and disagreement with the utility of actions.

Obstacles by Topic/Actions

Although many of the obstacles in table 8 appeared across several firewise topics, their prevalence and context varied widely by the specific actions for which they were reported. Tables 9 through 15 in appendix 2 display summary statistics and action-specific details on compliance and reported obstacles for each firewise topic. The following section describes how obstacles were related to individual topics/actions and provides examples of specific comments made by respondents.

Table 8—Frequency and proportion of respondents reporting obstacles to firewise recommendations

Obstacle code	Number of times obstacle was reported across all topics	Percentage of respondents reporting obstacle
Cost	125	21
Disagreement with recommendation	47	11
Lack of decision authority	36	6
Lack of knowledge	30	6
Lack of space	28	6
Aesthetic impact	26	5
Difficulty of completing action	25	5
Natural vegetation	24	5
Amount of work	24	5
Lack of time	19	4
Lack of physical ability	16	3
Neighbor issues	15	3
Terrain	15	3
Lack of adequate supply	15	3
Would require a remodel	12	3
Procrastination	8	2
Ecological impact	8	1
Lack of proper equipment	7	1
Laziness	4	1
Property layout	2	1

Access—

Actions suggested in the flyer dealt with making a home accessible for firefighters by having a driveway that is large enough, level, and clearly marked. The access flyer had the highest overall reported compliance (71 percent) and the smallest percentage of respondents reporting obstacles (17 percent) (table 9). Several respondents reported that issues with the amount of available space and the terrain on their property would make enlarging or reducing the grade of their driveway impossible. Examples include remarks such as "probably not enough room," "very rocky area," and "would require dynamite."

Water supply—

On average, 22 percent of respondents reported obstacles to implementing suggested water supply actions (table 10). The flyer recommends that residents maintain a minimum emergency water supply of 2,500 gallons and that this supply be easily seen and accessed by firefighters. Residents reporting obstacles suggested that the lack of availability of a large amount of water on their property and the high costs would prevent them from maintaining a 2,500-gallon supply. Specific comments included "Don't know if we could afford the generator," and "No access to such a supply."

Defensible space—

Only a few respondents reported obstacles to implementing actions related to keeping roof and gutters free of pine needles, debris, and overhanging limbs (2 to 4 percent) (table 11). More respondents reported obstacles to recommendations for extending the defensible space to 70 feet from a home and pruning all trees in this zone to at least 10 feet (30 percent and 14 percent, respectively). The perceived aesthetic impact of following these recommendations was the most common concern. Responses included "If I followed all the rules I might as well have a fire. The biggest tragedy a fire would have is the effect on my trees—not the house," and "When do I get a 'grant' for a Husqvarna chain saw?"

Trees and shrubs—

About one-third of respondents reported an obstacle for at least one of the recommendations for trees and shrubs (table 12). Actions related to plant arrangement and accumulation of flammable debris were met with concerns over maintaining natural vegetation and the amount of work associated with these tasks in a forested landscape. For example, one respondent suggested that "We don't want to disturb the natural vegetation and ecosystem with non native plants." Another remarked "The large size of the job—it's overwhelming." In regard to attending to trees in common areas between homes, several respondents suggested relations with the neighbors as an obstacle, e.g. "not all neighbors are as cooperative as they should be."

Construction and design—

Ten percent or fewer respondents reported obstacles to each individual suggestion for firewise construction and design (table 13). Recommendations related to using fire-resistant materials for windows, decks, vents, and the roof caused some respondents to make statements emphasizing the expense of materials, labor, etc. For example, one respondent characterized the obstacle as "a matter of economic deprivation," and another repeated that "this all costs money."

Interior safety—

Fewer than 5 percent of respondents reported obstacles to maintaining smoke detectors and fire extinguishers (table 14). Two actions suggested in this flyer drew concerns from many respondents. Installing a residential sprinkler system and drawing a floor plan to aid in evacuation were perceived, respectively, as too expensive and unnecessary. These two concerns resulted in the most obstacle comments for any of the individual actions (44 and 25, respectively). Responses included statements such as "cost of the system," "too expensive to do in a completed house," and "reviewing an escape plan is more effective than looking at it on a floor plan."

What to do when—
Fewer than 3 percent of respondents reported obstacles to having an escape plan, and knowing proper safety precautions during and after a specific wildfire event (table 15). The recommendation to have fire resistant materials to cover all windows in case of wildfire drew different comments suggesting several salient obstacles. The most prevalent among these were lack of storage space for the materials, cost of materials, and the amount/difficulty of work this action wound entail. Remarks included "lack of storage space," "labor available to do it," and "difficulty in covering windows 10 to 20 feet above ground level."

> The communication aspects of firewise programs are influenced by program goals, the effectiveness of message delivery, and audience characteristics, especially homeowners' orientations and attitudes toward fire risk and the agency involved in prevention and suppression.

Conclusions

Our results suggest a broader set of recommendations not strictly tested in our more limited individual studies and models. These deserve further study and discussion. The communication aspects of firewise programs are influenced by program goals, the effectiveness of message delivery, and audience characteristics, especially homeowners' orientations and attitudes toward fire risk and the agency involved in prevention and suppression. We suggest that agency attempts to change residents' responses to wildland fire threat can be enhanced by:

1. **Knowing the community**—Not all homeowners associations, neighborhoods, or communities share the same beliefs and attitudes regarding firewise behaviors. Understanding the differences in cognitive processes and psychological predictors will facilitate the design of effective communication strategies.

2. **Build trust, don't just rely on it**—Social trust in an agency can influence support for policies. Agencies, however, should not assume that the public trusts or even understands their decisions regarding wildfire management. Most work to date has been on the measurement and definition of trust. More attention needs to be placed on the practical effects of trust and how to maintain it. Efforts to build agency trust in a community will facilitate policy support and firewise compliance.

3. **Be flexible**—Although the psychological variables accounted for a substantial amount of variability in agency support and homeowner behavior, more than 50 percent of the variance remains unexplained. This suggests that decisionmakers should be flexible in their approaches dealing with individual communities. Programs often look to others for "success" and

emulate their actions. Our results suggest there are limits to an overly simplistic approach and attention to the differences between communities may be equally important.

4. **Engage, then persuade**—Develop a strategy to get homeowners to do something, as this seems to get the "biggest bang for the buck." Once they have started to do firewise actions, the likelihood is that other actions and attitude changes are likely to follow. Full compliance with all firewise actions is not likely given the costs and time involved, but getting homeowners to do some firewise action each year establishes the pattern of behavior and engenders support for the program in general.

Literature Cited

Absher, J.D.; Bright, A.D. 2004. Communication research in outdoor recreation and natural resources management. In: Manfredo, M.J.; Vaske, J.J.; Bruyere, B.L.; Field, D.R.; Brown, P.J., eds. Society and natural resources: a summary of knowledge. Jefferson, MO: Modern Litho: 117–126.

Absher, J.D.; Vaske, J.J. 2006. An analysis of homeowner and agency wildland fire mitigation strategies. In: Pedan, J.G.; Schuster, R.M., eds. Proceedings of the 2005 northeastern recreation research symposium. Gen. Tech. Rep. NE-341. Newtown Square, PA: U.S. Department of Agriculture, Forest Service, Northeastern Research Station: 231–236.

Absher, J.D.; Vaske, J.J. 2007a. Examining the sources of public support for wildland fire policies. Fire Management Today. 67(1): 35–39.

Absher, J.D.; Vaske, J.J. 2007b. Modeling public support for wildland fire policy. In: Reynolds, K.M.; Thomson, A.J.; Köhl, M.; Shannon, M.A.; Ray, D.; Rennolls, K., eds. Sustainable forestry: from monitoring and modeling to knowledge management and policy science. Wallingford, United Kingdom: CABI Press: 159–170 p.

Absher, J.D.; Vaske, J.J.; Bright, A.D. 2008. Basic beliefs, attitudes and social norms toward wildland fire management in southern California. In: Chavez, D.; Absher, J.; Winter, P., eds. Fire social science research from the Pacific Southwest Research Station: studies supported by national fire plan funds. Gen. Tech. Rep. PSW-209. Albany, CA: U.S. Department of Agriculture, Forest Service, Pacific Southwest Research Station: 45–56.

Biek, M.; Wood, W.; Chaiken, S. 1996. Working knowledge, cognitive processing, and attitudes: on the determinants of bias. Personality and Social Psychology Bulletin. 22: 547–556.

Bright, A.D.; Don Carlos, A.W.; Vaske, J.J.; Absher, J.D. 2007. Source credibility and effectiveness of firewise information. In: Burns, R.; Robinson, K., eds. Proceedings of the 2006 northeastern recreation research symposium. Gen. Tech. Rep. NRS-P-14. Newtown Square, PA: U.S. Department of Agriculture, Forest Service, Northern Research Station: 551–556.

Bright, A.D.; Vaske, J.J.; Kneeshaw, K.; Absher, J.D. 2003. Scale development of wildfire management basic beliefs. In: Jakes, P.J., comp. Homeowners, communities, and wildfire: science findings from the national fire plan. Gen. Tech. Rep. NC-231. St. Paul, MN: U.S. Department of Agriculture, Forest Service, North Central Research Station: 18–25.

Bright, A.D.; Vaske, J.J.; Kneeshaw, K.; Absher, J.D. 2005. Scale development of wildfire management basic beliefs. Australasian Parks and Leisure. 8(2): 44–48.

Cvetkovich, G.; Winter, P.L. 2003. Trust and social representations of the management of threatened and endangered species. Environment and Behavior. 35: 286–307.

Eagly, A.H.; Chaiken, S. 1993. The psychology of attitudes. New York: Harcourt Brace Jovanovich, Inc. 794 p.

Earle, T.C.; Cvetkovich, G.T. 1995. Social trust: toward a cosmopolitan society. Westport, CT: Praeger Press. 240 p.

Hafer, C.; Reynolds, K.; Obertynski, M. 1996. Message comprehensibility and persuasion: effects of complex language in counter attitudinal appeals to laypeople. Social Cognition. 14: 317–337.

Heesacker, M.H.; Petty, R.E.; Cacioppo, J.T. 1983. Field dependence and attitude change: source credibility can alter persuasion by affecting message-relevant thinking. Journal of Personality. 51: 653–666.

Homer, P.M.; Kahle, L.R. 1988. A structural equation test of the value-attitude-behavior hierarchy. Journal of Personality and Social Psychology. 54: 638–646.

Manfredo, M.J.; Bright, A.D. 1991. A model for assessing the effects of communication on recreationists. Journal of Leisure Research. 23: 1–20.

Petty, R.E.; Cacioppo, J.T. 1986. The Elaboration Likelihood Model. In: Berkowitz, L., ed. Advances in experimental social psychology. New York: Academic Press. 19: 123–205.

Rokeach, M. 1973. The nature of human values. New York: The Free Press. 438 p.

Siegrist, M.; Cvetkovich, G.; Roth, C. 2000. Salient value similarity, social trust, and risk/benefit perception. Risk Analysis. 20(3): 353–362.

Siegrist, M.; Cvetkovich, G.; Gutscher, H. 2001. Shared values, social trust, and the perception of geographic cancer clusters. Risk Analysis. 21(6): 1047–1053.

Stern, P.C. 2000. Toward a coherent theory of environmentally significant behavior. Journal of Social Issues. 56(3): 407–424.

Toman, E.L.; Shindler, B.; Absher, J.D.; McCaffrey, S. 2008. Post fire communications: the influence of site visits on local support. Journal of Forestry. January/February: 25–30.

Vaske, J.J. 2008. Survey research and analysis: applications in parks, recreation and human dimensions. State College, PA: Venture Publishing, Inc. 658 p.

Vaske, J.J.; Absher, J.D.; Bright, A.D. 2007a. Salient value similarity, social trust and attitudes toward wildland fire management strategies. Human Ecology Review. 14(2): 223–232.

Vaske, J.J.; Absher, J.D.; Bright, A.D. 2007b. Salient value similarity, social trust and attitudes toward wildland fire management strategies. In: Burns, R.; Robinson, K., eds. Proceedings of the 2006 northeastern recreation research symposium. Gen. Tech. Rep. NRS-P-14. Newtown Square, PA: U.S. Department of Agriculture, Forest Service, Northern Research Station: 557–565.

Vaske, J.J.; Donnelly, M.P. 1999. A value-attitude-behavior model predicting wildland voting intentions. Society and Natural Resources. 12: 523–537.

Whittaker, D.; Vaske, J.J.; Manfredo, M.J. 2006. Specificity and the cognitive hierarchy: value orientations and the acceptability of urban wildlife management actions. Society and Natural Resources. 19: 515–530.

Winter, G.; Vogt, C.A.; McCaffrey, S. 2004. Examining social trust in fuels management strategies. Journal of Forestry. September: 8–15.

Wood, W.; Kallgren, C.A. 1988. Communicator attributes and persuasion: recipient access to attitude-relevant information in memory. Personality and Social Psychology Bulletin. 14: 172–182.

Appendix 1: Description of Studies

Study 1

Data for this study were obtained from a mail survey sent to individuals who had visited Arapaho-Roosevelt National Forest (Colorado), Mount Baker-Snoqualmie National Forest (Washington), and the San Bernardino National Forest (California). These three forests were chosen because of their close proximity to an urban setting (Denver, Seattle, and Los Angeles, respectively).

The study population consisted of individuals over the age of 18 who visited one of the three forests. A random sample of forest user names and mailing addresses from each of the three forests was collected from an onsite survey conducted in the summer of 2001. For the three forests combined, 3,131 interviews were completed onsite; 2,706 usable names and addresses were received for the followup mail survey.

Mail survey administration—
An initial version of the mail survey was pretested using a sample (n = 200) of Colorado State University students during fall 2001. The pretest suggested several minor revisions that were incorporated into the instrument before conducting the mail survey. Four mailings were used to administer the survey beginning at the end of January 2002. Participants first received the 12-page questionnaire, a prepaid postage return envelope, and a personalized cover letter explaining the study and requesting their participation. Ten days after the initial mailing, a reminder postcard was sent to participants. A second complete mailing (questionnaire, prepaid postage return envelope and cover letter) was sent to nonrespondents 10 days after the postcard reminder. To further increase response rate, a third complete mailing was sent 1 month following the second complete mailing. A total of 1,288 mail surveys were returned with an overall response rate of 51 percent (1,288 returned/[2,706 sent − 176 nondeliverables]). Response rates for individual forests were Arapaho-Roosevelt 56 percent (469 returned/[890 sent − 53 nondeliverables]), Mount Baker-Snoqualmie 54 percent (498 returned/[987 sent − 70 nondeliverables]), and San Bernardino 41 percent (321 returned/[829 sent − 53 nondeliverables]).

As a check on potential nonresponse bias, onsite survey information was compared for those who returned the mail survey versus those who did not. For all the variables on the onsite survey (the dependent variables), the Hedge's g effect sizes were < 0.2, indicating only a "minimal" relationship (Vaske 2008). Nonresponse bias was thus not considered to be a problem and the data were not weighted.

Study 2

The population for this study consisted of landowners over the age of 18 who reside in the rural areas (Census 2000) of six Colorado counties (Boulder, Clear Creek, Gilpin, Grand, Jackson, and Larimer). A random sample of resident names and addresses was purchased from a commercial sampling firm in the summer of 2004.

Mail survey administration—

Four mailings were used to administer the survey beginning at the end of May 2004. Residents first received the 12-page questionnaire, a prepaid postage return envelope and a personalized cover letter explaining the study and requesting their participation. Ten days after the initial mailing, a reminder postcard was sent to participants. A second complete mailing (questionnaire, prepaid postage return envelope and cover letter) was sent to nonrespondents 10 days after the postcard reminder. To further increase the response rate, a third complete mailing was sent 1 month following the second complete mailing. A total of 532 completed surveys were returned with an overall response rate of 47 percent (532 returned/ 1,200 sent – 56 nondeliverables).

As a check on potential nonresponse bias, a telephone survey was conducted of nonresponse residences (n = 100). Selected key issues (perceived effectiveness, approval, and aesthetic impacts of prescribed burning and mechanical thinning) were addressed in the telephone survey. Differences between respondents and nonrespondents on these central topics were "minimal" (Hedges' g effect sizes < 0.2) (Vaske 2008). Thus, nonresponse bias was not considered to be a problem and the data were not weighted.

Study 3

Data for this experiment were obtained from a mail survey. An introductory post-card, two full questionnaire mailings, and a reminder postcard were sent out during June and July, 2005. The study area included seven counties in northern Colorado (Jackson, Grand, Gilpin, Clear Creek, Larimer, Boulder, Jefferson). Residences in Jackson, Grand, Gilpin, and Clear Creek Counties were considered to be entirely within the WUI. In Larimer, Boulder, and Jefferson Counties, only selected areas (e.g., mountain foothills communities) were included in the sampling frame. Using these geographical boundaries, a random sample of 1,200 residences was purchased from a commercial sampling firm.

Mail survey administration—

Of the 1,200 surveys mailed to households, 149 were undeliverable. From the remaining 1,051 households, 402 usable surveys were received for an overall response rate of 38 percent. Shortened nonresponse surveys were sent to a random sample of 250 residences who had not returned the original survey for the purpose of comparing respondents with nonrespondents. Of the 250 nonresponse surveys mailed out, 71 were returned for use in the nonresponse analysis. No significant differences were found between the respondent and nonrespondent surveys and thus, the data were not weighted.

Experimental design—

Prior to mailing the questionnaire, households were randomly placed into one of three groups. Each group was told that the information was from one of the following sources: USDA Forest Service, Colorado State Forest Service, or a local fire department organization. Each household received a survey that included flyers related to each of three of the seven firewise topics. An orthogonal design procedure was conducted to determine what combination of three topics would be included in each survey. This was done to make sure that each topic was included an equal number of times across all surveys.

Variables measured—

The questionnaire included measures of source credibility, message clarity, message elaboration, and behavior change. Respondents rated the credibility/trust of one information source, which was provided randomly from three potential sources as above. Credibility was measured as an index of four 7-point items. Message clarity was addressed by asking respondent to evaluate how difficult the information provided was to understand. Responses were coded on a 5-point scale. For message elaboration, respondents were asked how carefully they had read the information provided them (5-point scale). Finally, respondents were asked, on a 5-point scale, how likely it was that the information would change their behavior regarding specific firewise actions.

Appendix 2: Firewise Actions

Table 9—Respondents' self-reported compliance and obstacles for recommended "Access" actions (n = 127)

Action	Percentage in compliance[a]	Percentage reporting obstacles	Most commonly reported obstacles	Number of times obstacle reported
Your driveway has enough area for emergency vehicles to enter and turn around.	73	13	Lack of space	8
			Cost	4
			Difficulty	3
Your address is posted at the entrance of your driveway or other easily seen location.	80	3	Neighbor concerns	2
			Procrastination	2
Your driveway is not too steep for emergency equipment to get to your home.	61	7	Terrain	4
			Difficulty	3
			Cost	4

Summary statistics:

Average percentage of respondents in compliance across all actions	71
Percentage of respondents who reported obstacles for one or more actions[b]	17
Total number of obstacles reported across all actions[c]	44

[a] Percentage in compliance represents the number of respondents reporting that the action was "already done" on their property as a proportion of the total that responded to the "Access" questions.

[b] Some respondents reported obstacles for more than one action, thus this percentage is not a sum of the percentage reporting obstacles for each of the individual actions.

[c] This is the total number of obstacles reported for all of the "Access" actions. Only the most common obstacles for each action are reported in the right-hand column above; thus they do not sum to this total.

Table 10—Respondents' self-reported compliance and obstacles for recommended "Water Supply" actions (n = 142)

Action	Percentage in compliance[a]	Percentage reporting obstacles (for each action)	Most commonly reported obstacles	Number of times obstacle reported
Your property has access to a minimum supply of 2,500 gallons of emergency water.	45	19	Lack of supply	10
			Cost	9
			Lack of space	5
Your water supply is accessible by firefighters.	60	9	Cost	5
			Lack of supply	3
			Terrain	2
			Lack of knowledge	2
Your water supply valve is easily seen from the nearest road.	42	8	Cost	4
			Lack of knowledge	2
			Lack of supply	2

Summary statistics:

Average percentage of respondents in compliance across all actions	49
Percentage of respondents who reported obstacles for one or more actions[b]	22
Total number of obstacles reported across all actions[c]	65

[a] Percentage in compliance represents the number of respondents reporting that the action was "already done" on their property as a proportion of the total that responded to the "Water Supply" questions.

[b] Some respondents reported obstacles for more than one action, thus this percentage is not a sum of the percentage reporting obstacles for each of the individual actions.

[c] This is the total number of obstacles reported for all of the "Water Supply" actions. Only the most common obstacles for each action are reported in the right-hand column above, thus they do not sum to this total.

Table 11—Respondents' self-reported compliance and obstacles for recommended "Defensible Space" actions (n = 118)

Action	Percentage in compliance[a]	Percentage reporting obstacles (for each action)	Most commonly reported obstacles	Number of times obstacle reported
Your defensible space extends at least 70 feet around your home.	43	30	Aesthetic impact	11
			Cost	8
			Lack decision authority	6
			Lack of time	3
Your roof and gutters are free of pine needles, leaves, and other debris.	69	2	Lack of physical ability	2
Branches that extend over your roof have been trimmed.	56	4	Cost	2
Trees within your defensible space have branches pruned to at least 10 feet above the ground.	45	14	Aesthetic impact	5
			Lack of decision authority	4
			Cost	2
			Lack of equipment	2

Summary statistics:

Average percentage of respondents in compliance across all actions	53
Percentage of respondents who reported obstacles for one or more actions[b]	34
Total number of obstacles reported across all actions[c]	66

[a] Percentage in compliance represents the number of respondents reporting that the action was "already done" on their property as a proportion of the total that responded to the "Defensible Space" questions.

[b] Some respondents reported obstacles for more than one action, thus this percentage is not a sum of the percentage reporting obstacles for each of the individual actions.

[c] This is the total number of obstacles reported for all of the "Defensible Space" actions. Only the most common obstacles for each action are reported in the right-hand column above, thus they do not sum to this total.

Table 12—Respondents' self-reported compliance and obstacles for recommended "Trees and Shrubs" actions (n = 129)

Action	Percentage in compliance[a]	Percentage reporting obstacles (for each action)	Most commonly reported obstacles	Number of times obstacle reported
Plants at your residence do not accumulate dead branches, needles, leaves, or debris.	46	25	Natural vegetation	14
			Amount of work	8
			Cost	5
Plants at your residence are arranged in small clusters rather than large masses.	60	11	Natural vegetation	6
			Lack of time	2
			Lack of knowledge	2
			Cost	2
Plants and trees in common areas between homes have been cleared or pruned.	48	13	Neighbor concerns	7
			Natural vegetation	3
			Cost	3
You have insured that there are few or no trees under or near electrical lines.	57	9	Lack of decision authority	3
			Cost	3
Summary statistics:				
Average percentage of respondents in compliance across all actions			53	
Percentage of respondents who reported obstacles for one or more actions[b]			34	
Total number of obstacles reported across all actions[c]			101	

[a] Percentage in compliance represents the number of respondents reporting that the action was "already done" on their property as a proportion of the total that responded to the "Trees and Shrubs" questions.

[b] Some respondents reported obstacles for more than one action, thus this percentage is not a sum of the percentage reporting obstacles for each of the individual actions.

[c] This is the total number of obstacles reported for all of the "Trees and Shrubs" actions. Only the most common obstacles for each action are reported in the right-hand column above, thus they do not sum to this total.

Table 13—Respondents' self-reported compliance and obstacles for recommended "Construction and Design" actions (n = 146)

Action	Percentage in compliance[a]	Percentage reporting obstacles (for each action)	Most commonly reported obstacles	Number of times obstacle reported
Your windows and sliding glass doors are made of multipaned glass.	81	10	Cost	11
			Lack of decision authority	2
			Would require r emodel	2
Areas under your deck or balcony are enclosed with fire-resistive materials or otherwise kept free of vegetation.	50	9	Cost	7
			Aesthetic impact	2
			Amount of work	2
			Lack of knowledge	2
			Would require remodel	2
Your exterior attic, soffit, and underfloor vents are covered in wire mesh.	42	10	Cost	4
			Lack of knowledge	3
Your roof is constructed using appropriate roofing materials (e.g., asphalt shingles, slate or clay tile, or metal).	92	2	Would require remodel	2
			Cost	2

Summary statistics:

Average percentage of respondents in compliance across all actions	66
Percentage of respondents who reported obstacles for one or more actions[b]	24
Total number of obstacles reported across all actions[c]	57

[a] Percentage in compliance represents the number of respondents reporting that the action was "already done" on their property as a proportion of the total that responded to the "Construction and Design" questions.

[b] Some respondents reported obstacles for more than one action, thus this percentage is not a sum of the percentage reporting obstacles for each of the individual actions.

[c] This is the total number of obstacles reported for all of the "Construction and Design" actions. Only the most common obstacles for each action are reported in the right-hand column above, thus they do not sum to this total.

Table 14—Respondents' self-reported compliance and obstacles for recommended "Interior Safety" actions (n = 142)

Action	Percentage in compliance[a]	Percentage reporting obstacles (for each action)	Most commonly reported obstacles	Number of times obstacle reported
Your home is equipped with a residential sprinkler system.	2	39	Cost	44
			Would require remodel	4
			Disagree with recommendation	3
			Lack of decision authority	3
Your home is equipped with working smoke detectors outside of each sleeping area or on every level.	91	1	Procrastination	1
Your home contains a fire extinguisher on each floor level.	66	4	Disagree with recommendation	3
			Cost	2
You have a floor plan of your home that marks two ways out of every room.	35	19	Disagree with recommendation	25

Summary statistics:

Average percentage of respondents in compliance across all actions	49
Percentage of respondents who reported obstacles for one or more actions[b]	42
Total number of obstacles reported across all actions[c]	101

[a] Percentage in compliance represents the number of respondents reporting that the action was "already done" on their property as a proportion of the total that responded to the "Interior Safety" questions.

[b] Some respondents reported obstacles for more than one action, thus this percentage is not a sum of the percentage reporting obstacles for each of the individual actions.

[c] This is the total number of obstacles reported for all of the "Interior Safety" actions. Only the most common obstacles for each action are reported in the right-hand column above, thus they do not sum to this total.

Table 15—Respondents' self-reported compliance and obstacles for recommended "What to Do When" actions (n = 135)

Action	Percentage in compliance[a]	Percentage reporting obstacles (for each action)	Most commonly reported obstacles	Number of times obstacle reported
You have a plan of action (escape plan) in case a fire approaches your home.	52	2	Disagree with recommendation	1
You have fire-resistant material to cover windows or other openings in case of a fire.	13	24	Lack of space (for storage)	8
			Cost	6
			Amount of work	5
			Disagree with recommendation	5
			Difficulty	5
			Lack of knowledge	5
You know safety procedures if you are trapped by fire while trying to evacuate.	39	2	Lack of knowledge	1
			Procrastination	1
You know proper procedures for inspecting your home for burning embers after a wildfire passes.	32	3	Lack of knowledge	2
			Lack of physical ability	2

Summary statistics:

Average percentage of respondents in compliance across all actions	34
Percentage of respondents who reported obstacles for one or more actions[b]	27
Total number of obstacles reported across all actions[c]	52

[a] Percentage in compliance represents the number of respondents reporting that the action was "already done" on their property as a proportion of the total that responded to the "What to Do When" questions.

[b] Some respondents reported obstacles for more than one action, thus this percentage is not a sum of the percentage reporting obstacles for each of the individual actions.

[c] This is the total number of obstacles reported for all of the "What to Do When" actions. Only the most common obstacles for each action are reported in the right-hand column above, thus they do not sum to this total.